I,

....

am here to unleash my unlimited creativity!

Hey there, before you start...
I'd like to share a few tips with you

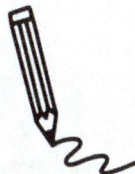

This is your playground,
the only thing you need is a PEN

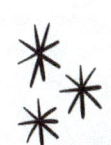

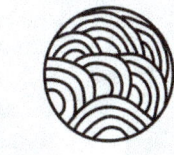

You may doodle, draw, outline, adding
zentangle pattern......all as you wish

Soak yourself into the imaginative
realm, unleash your inner creativity!

"I am safe to explore my creative side and express my creative self."

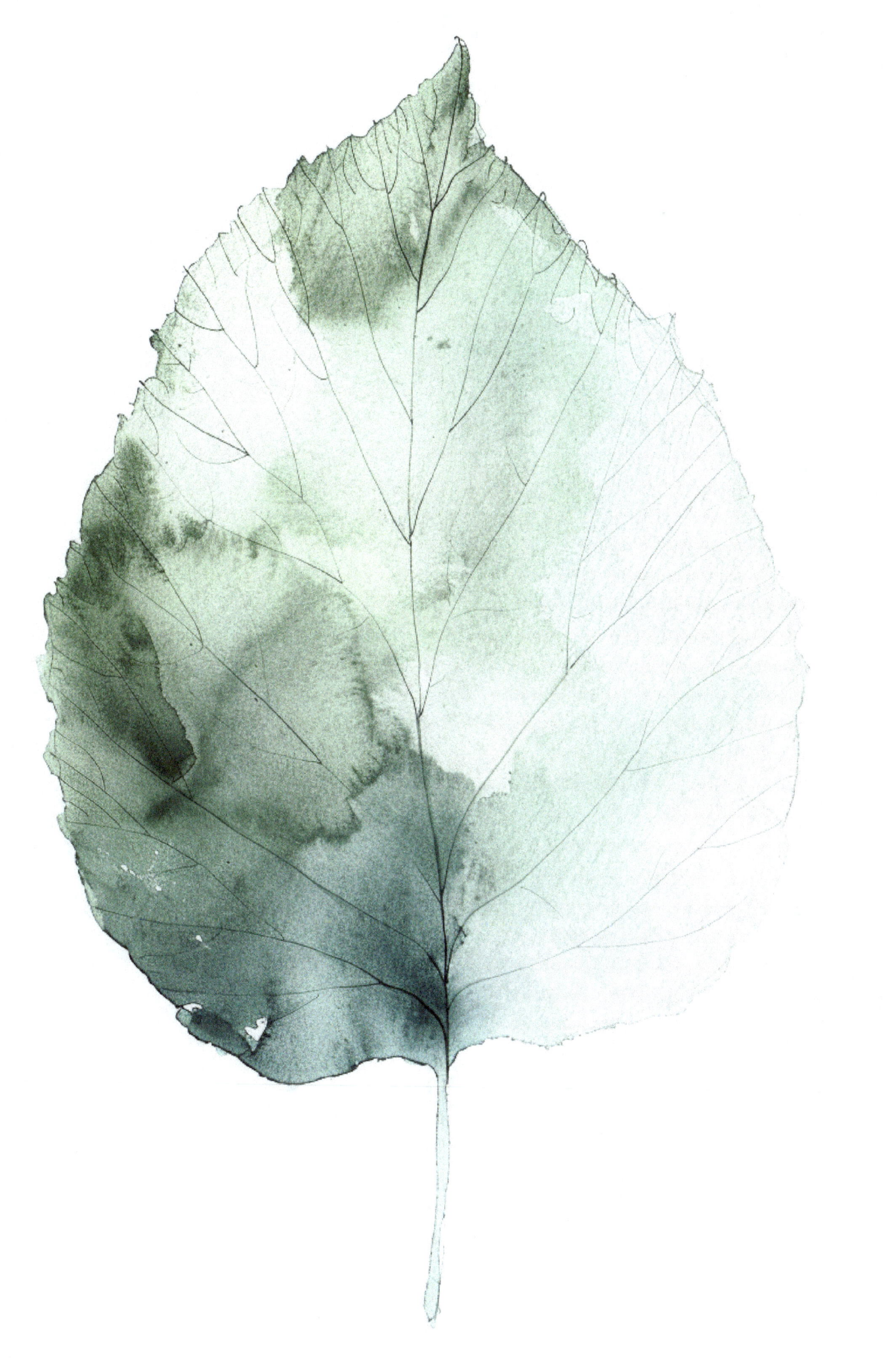

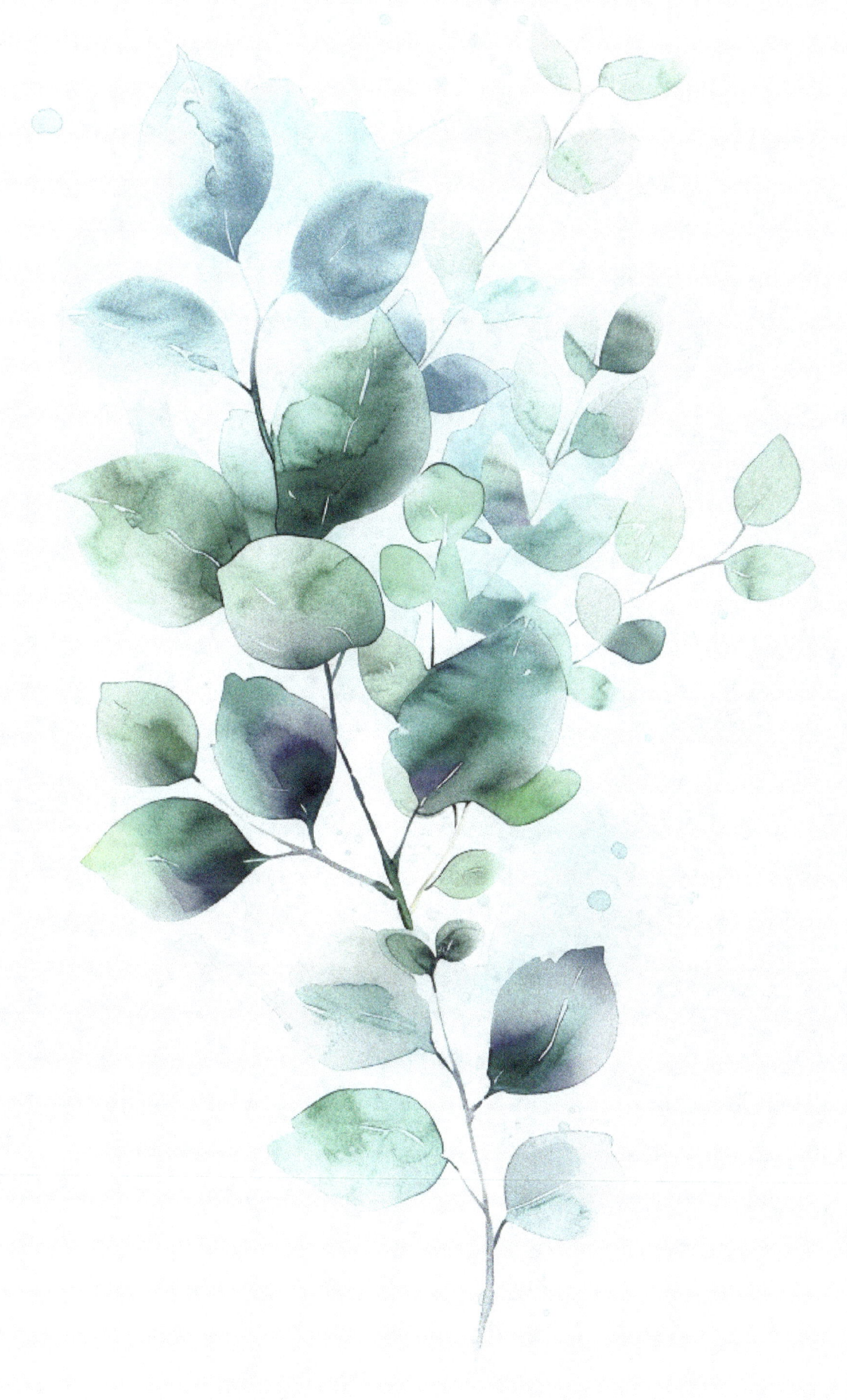

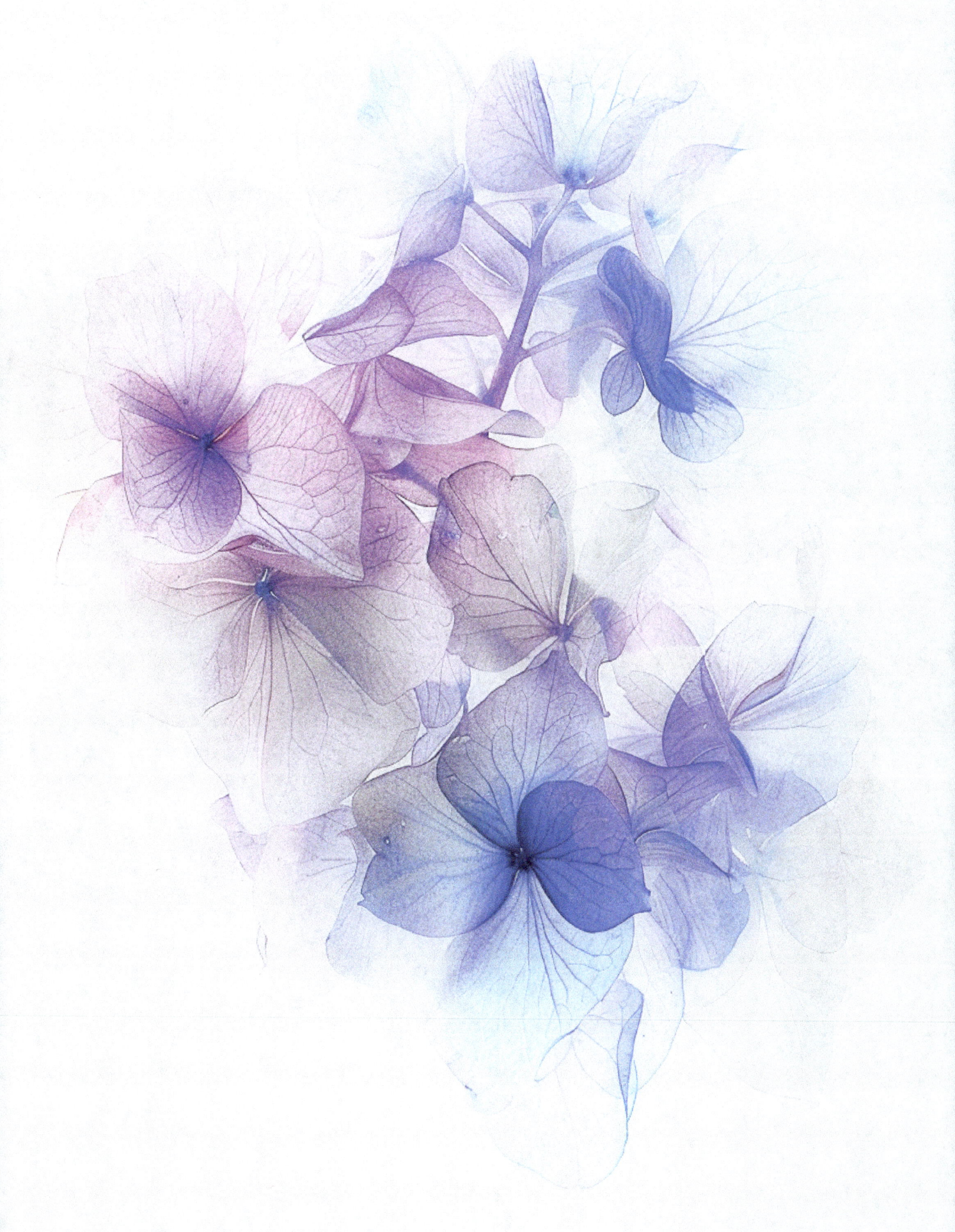

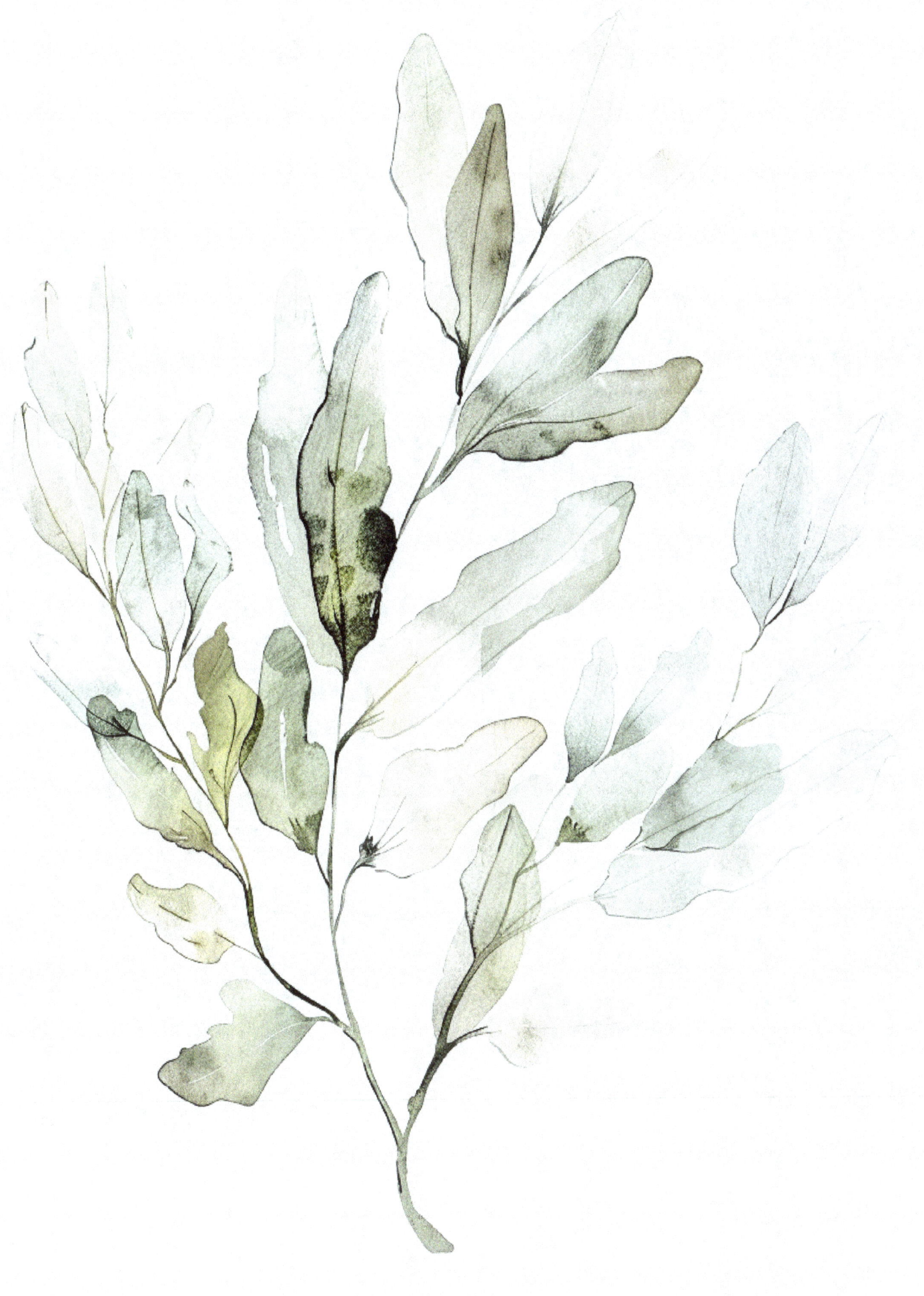

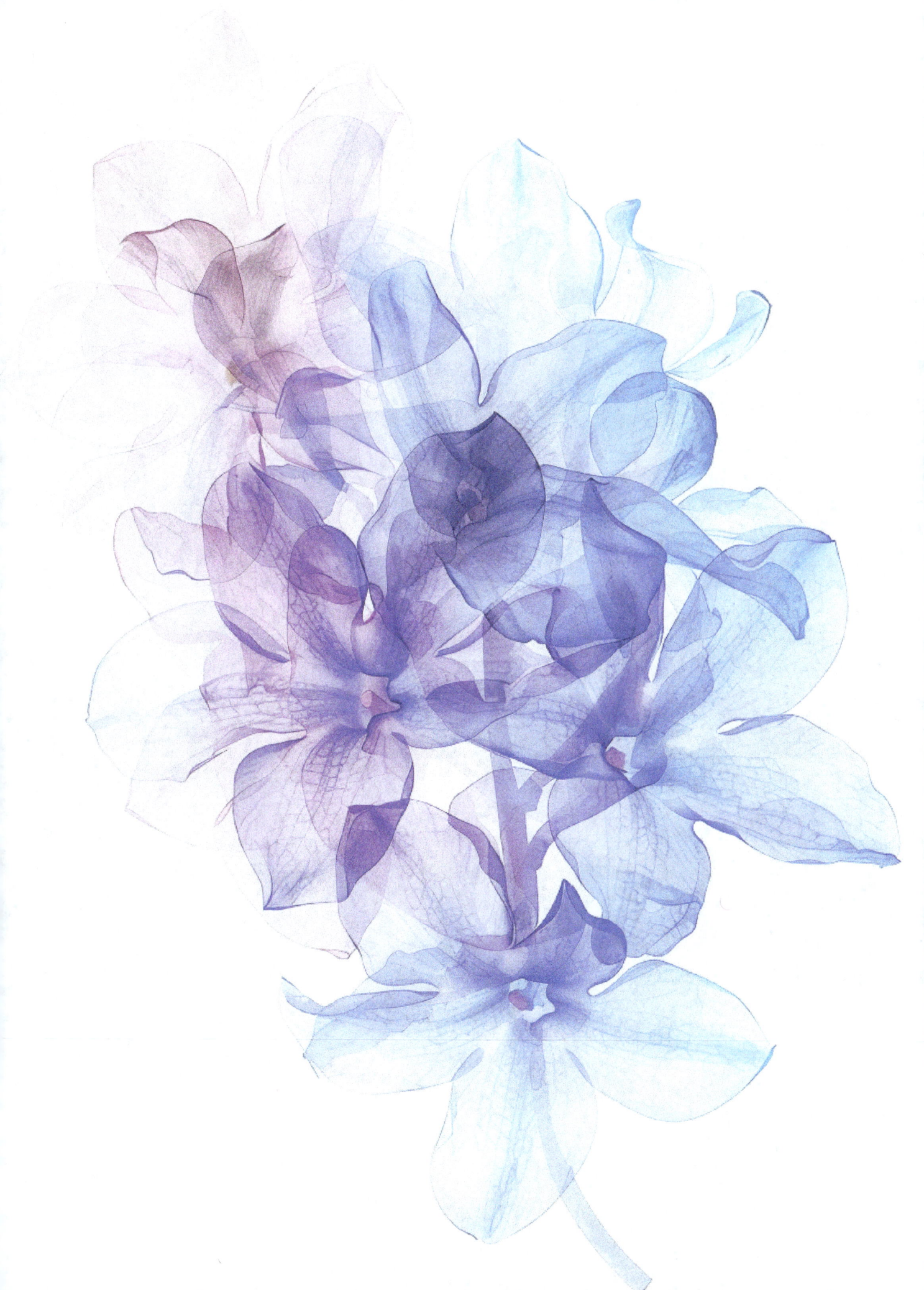

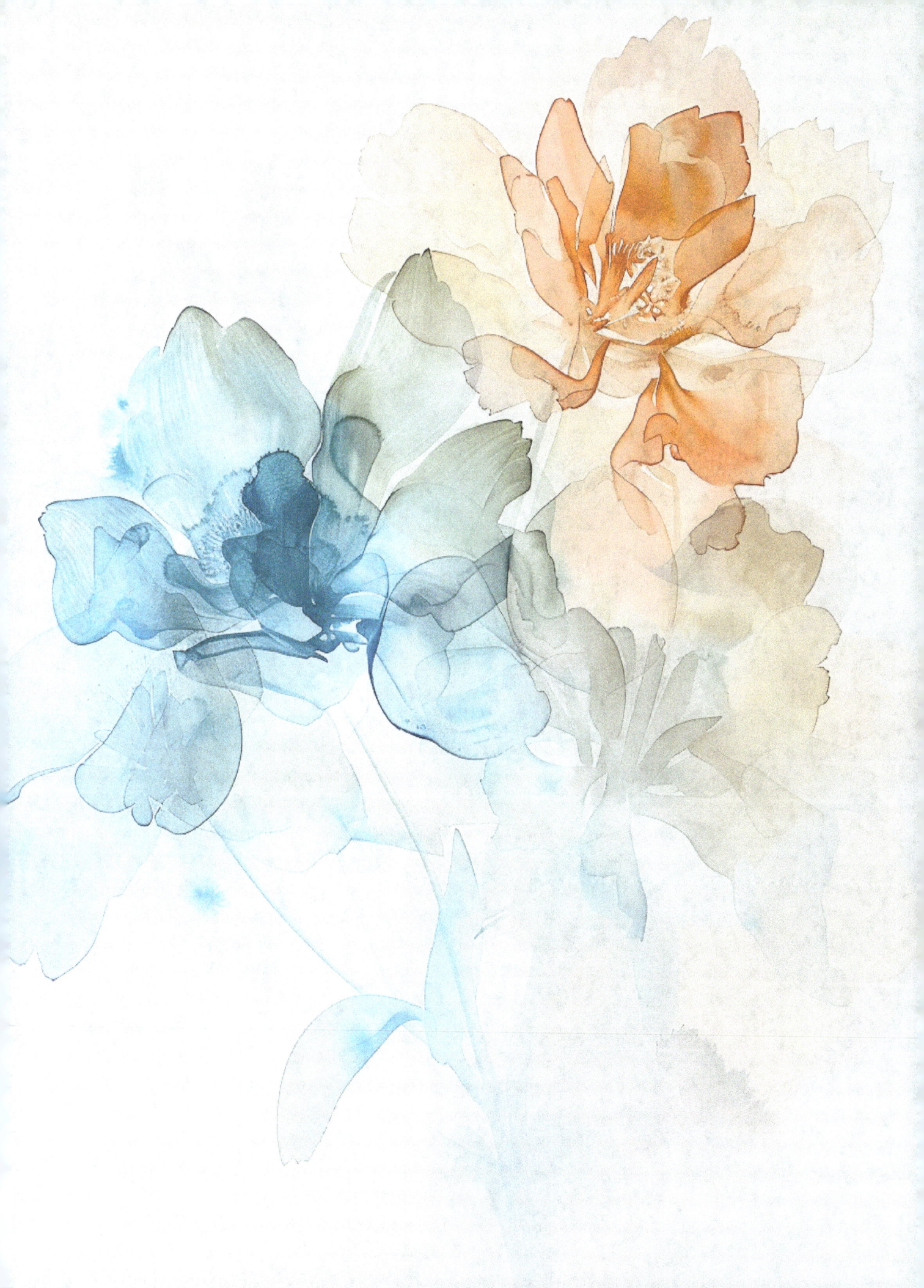

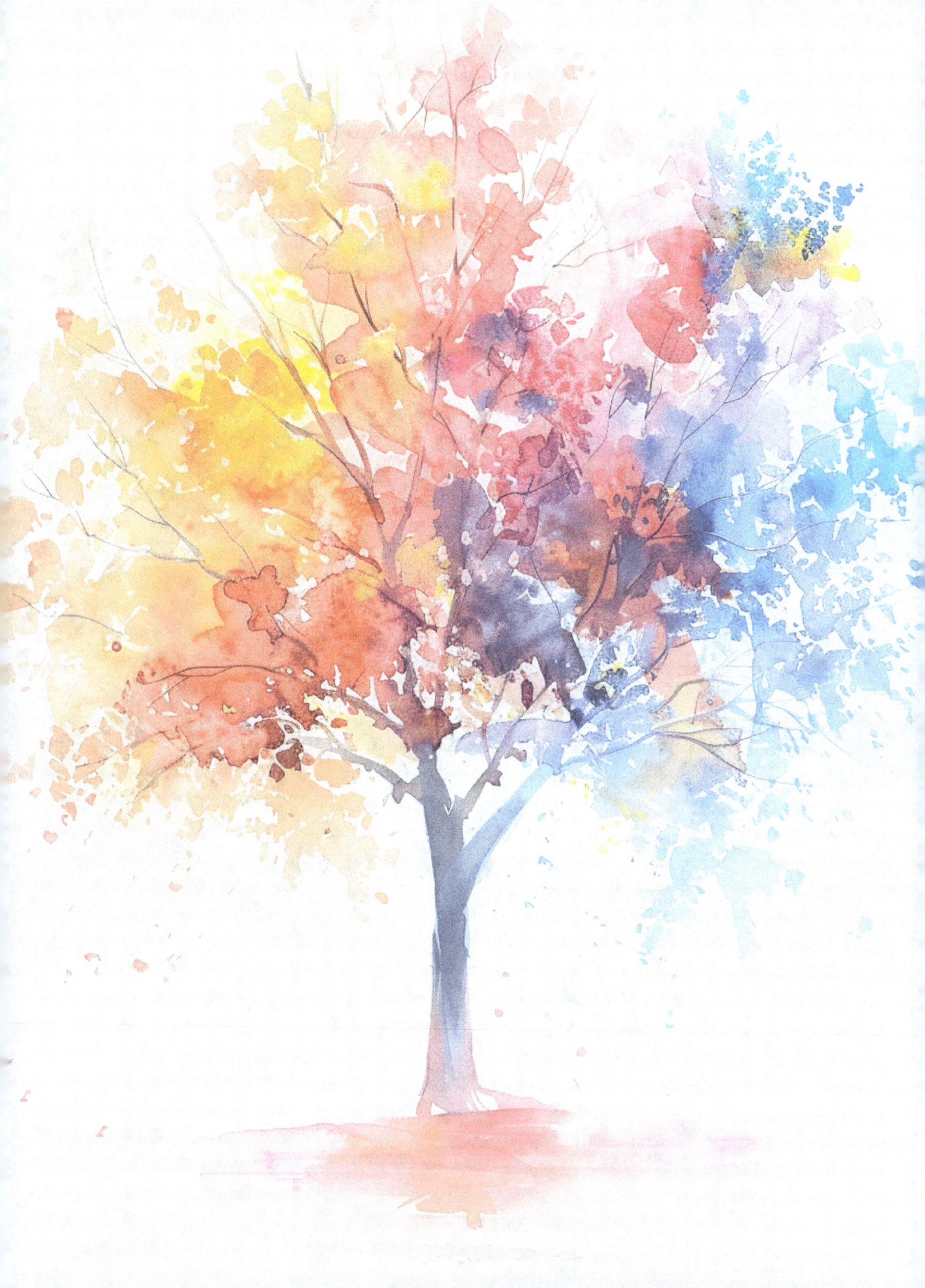

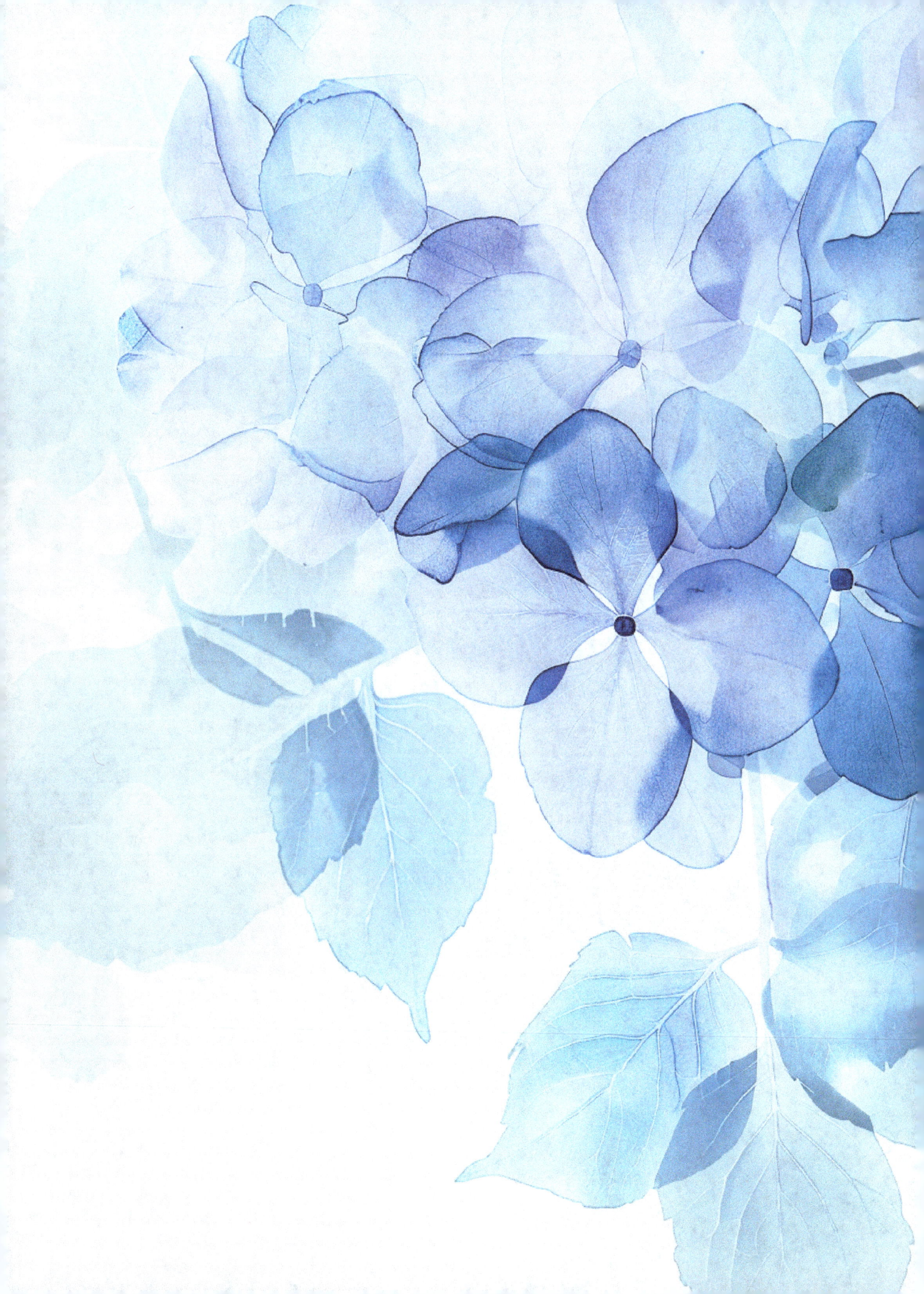

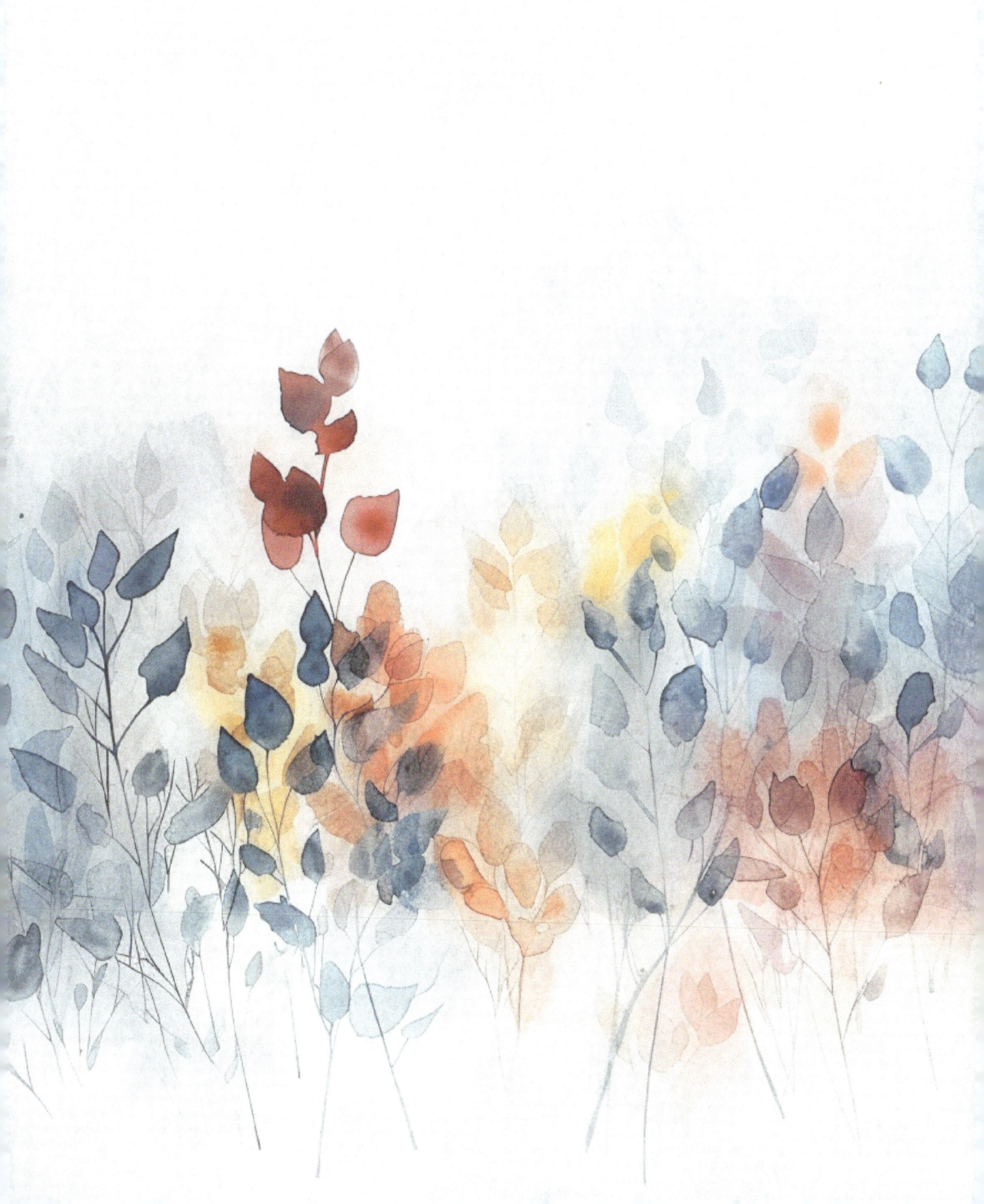

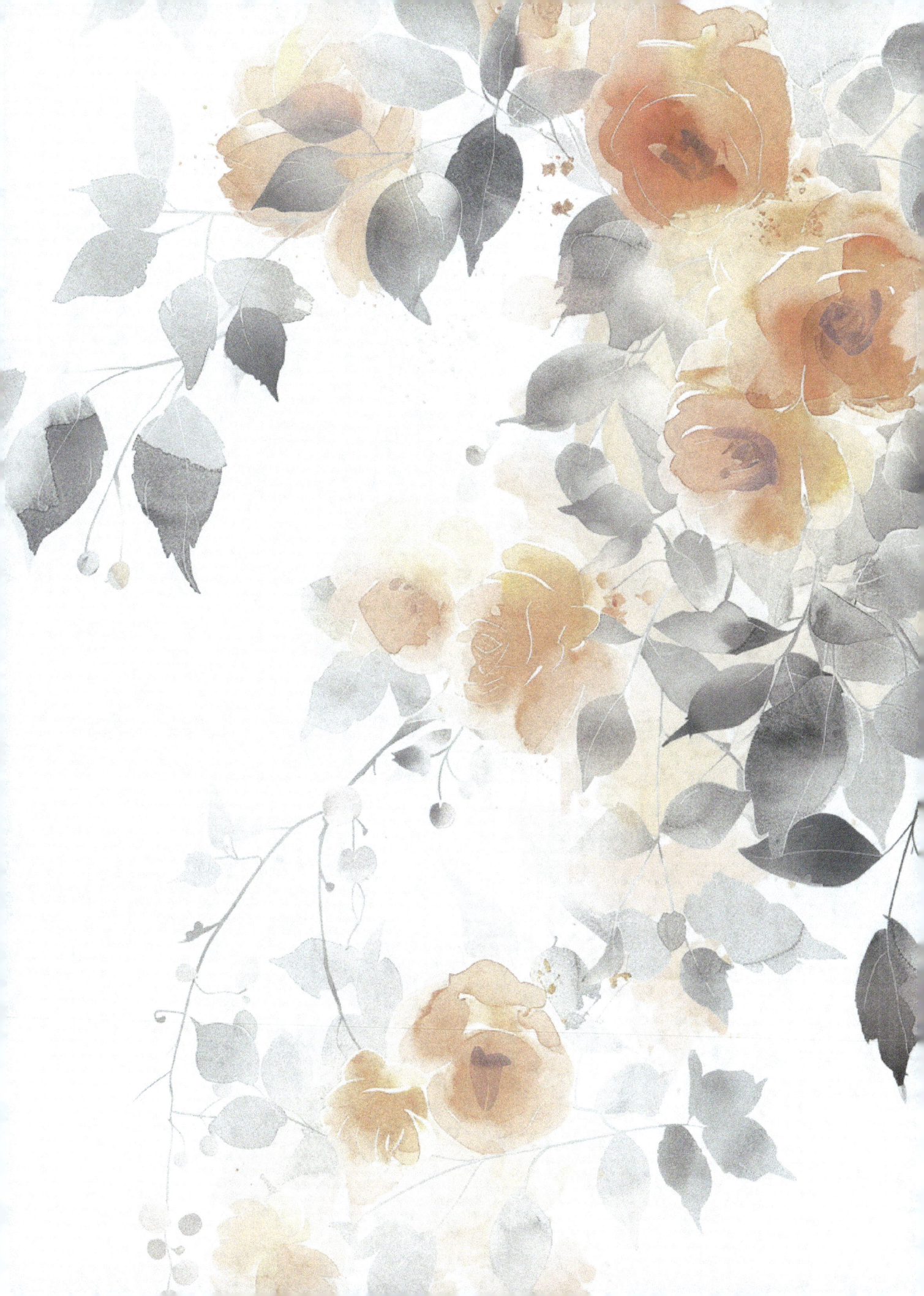

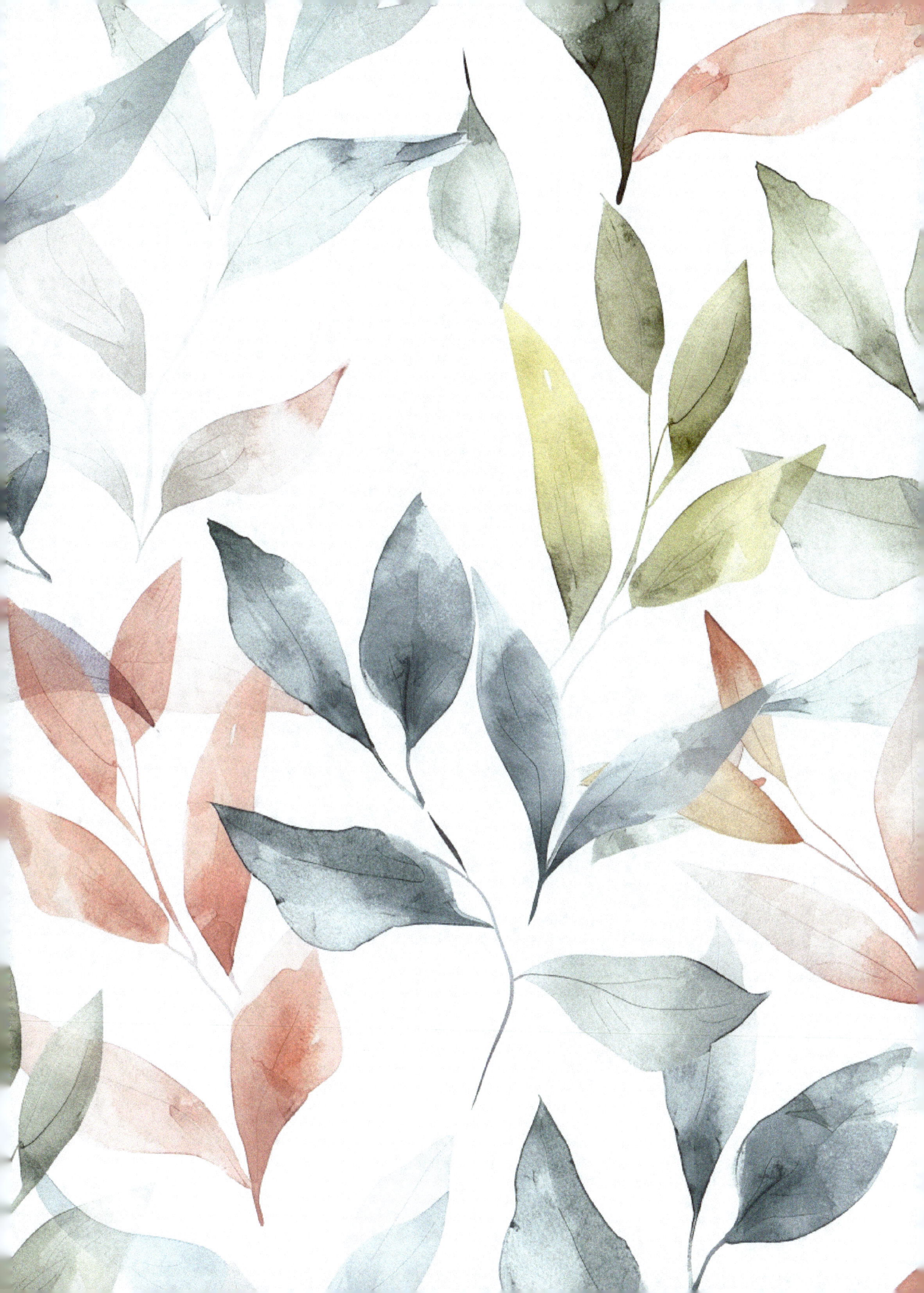

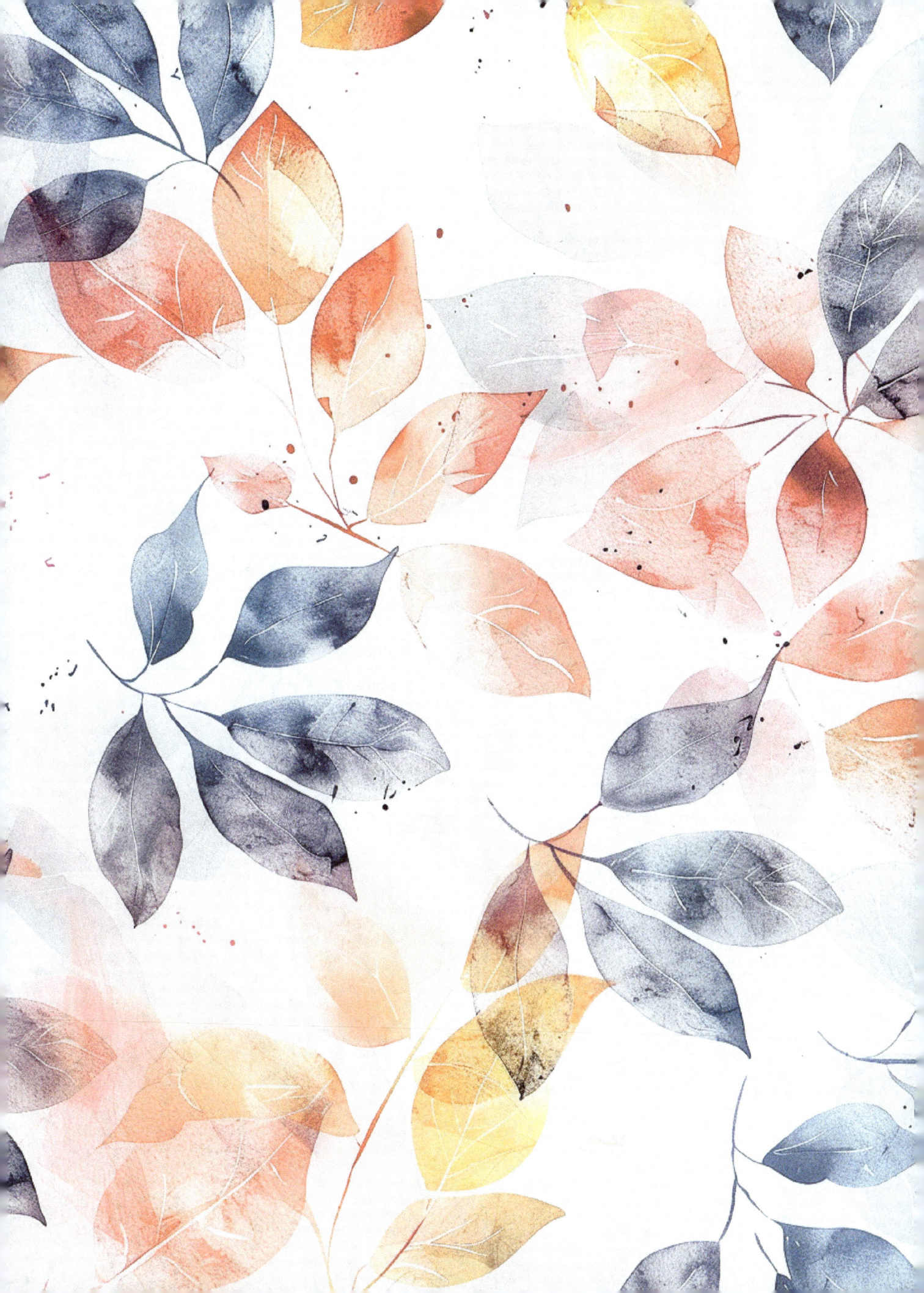

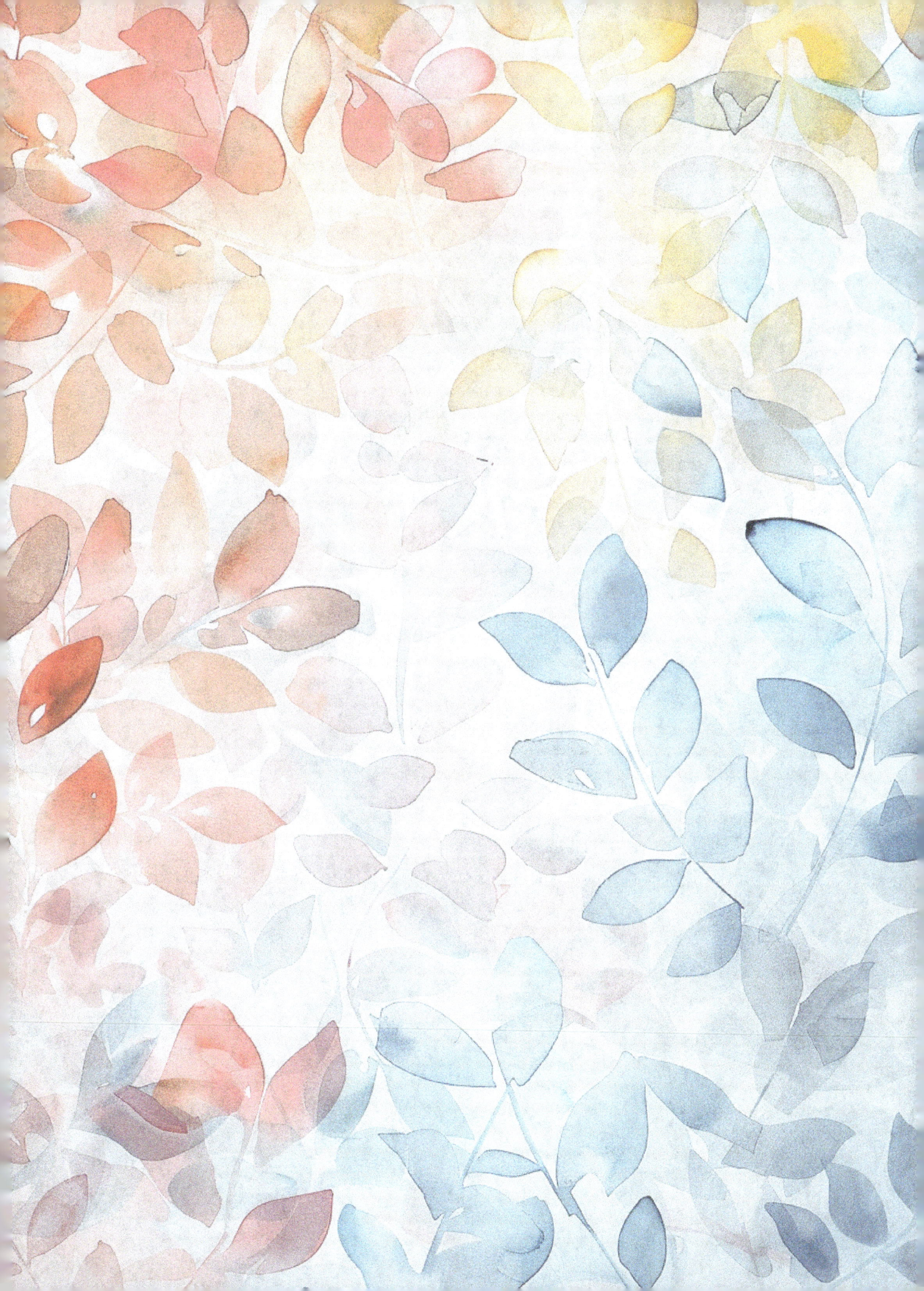

Creativity flows through me like a river.

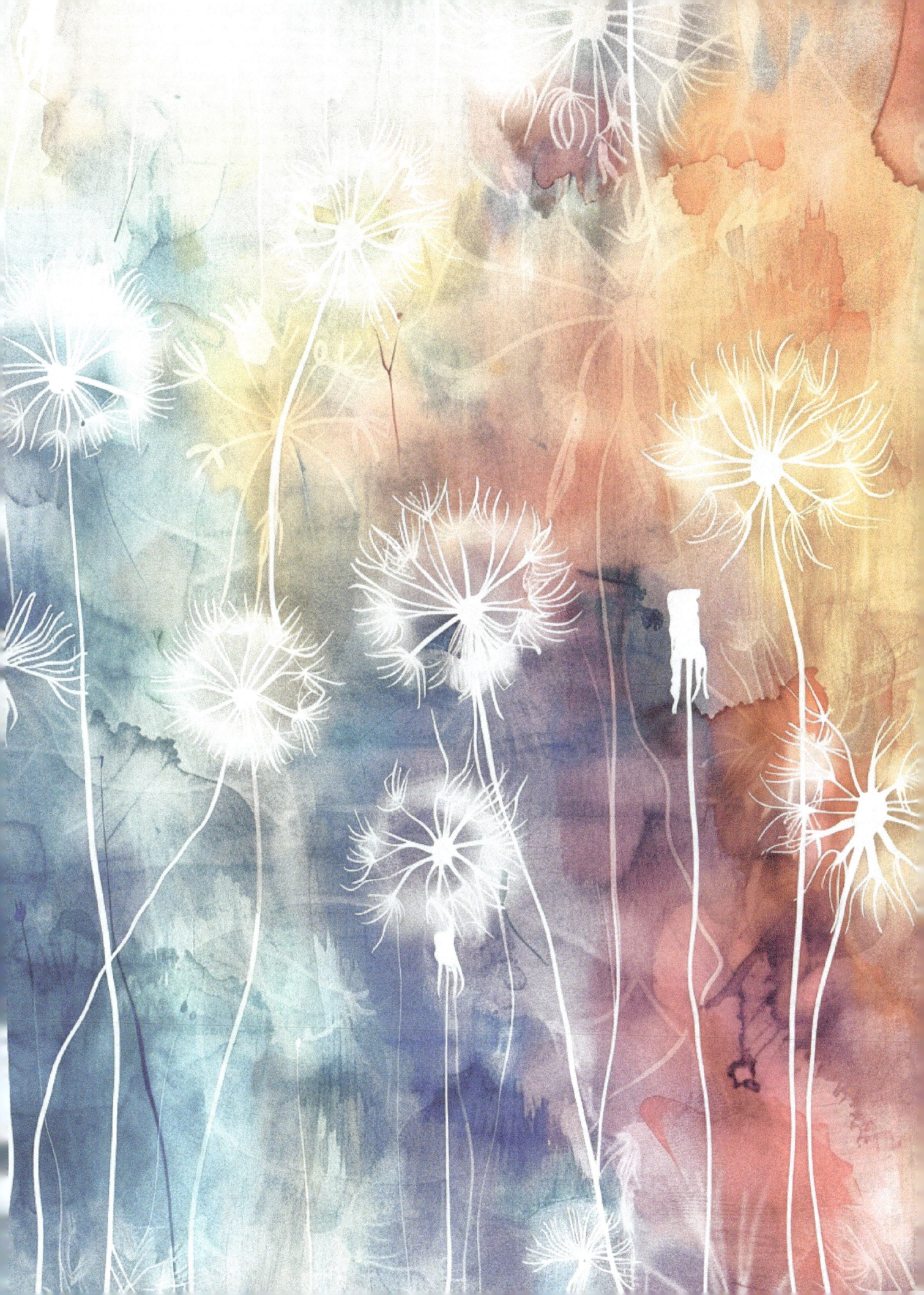

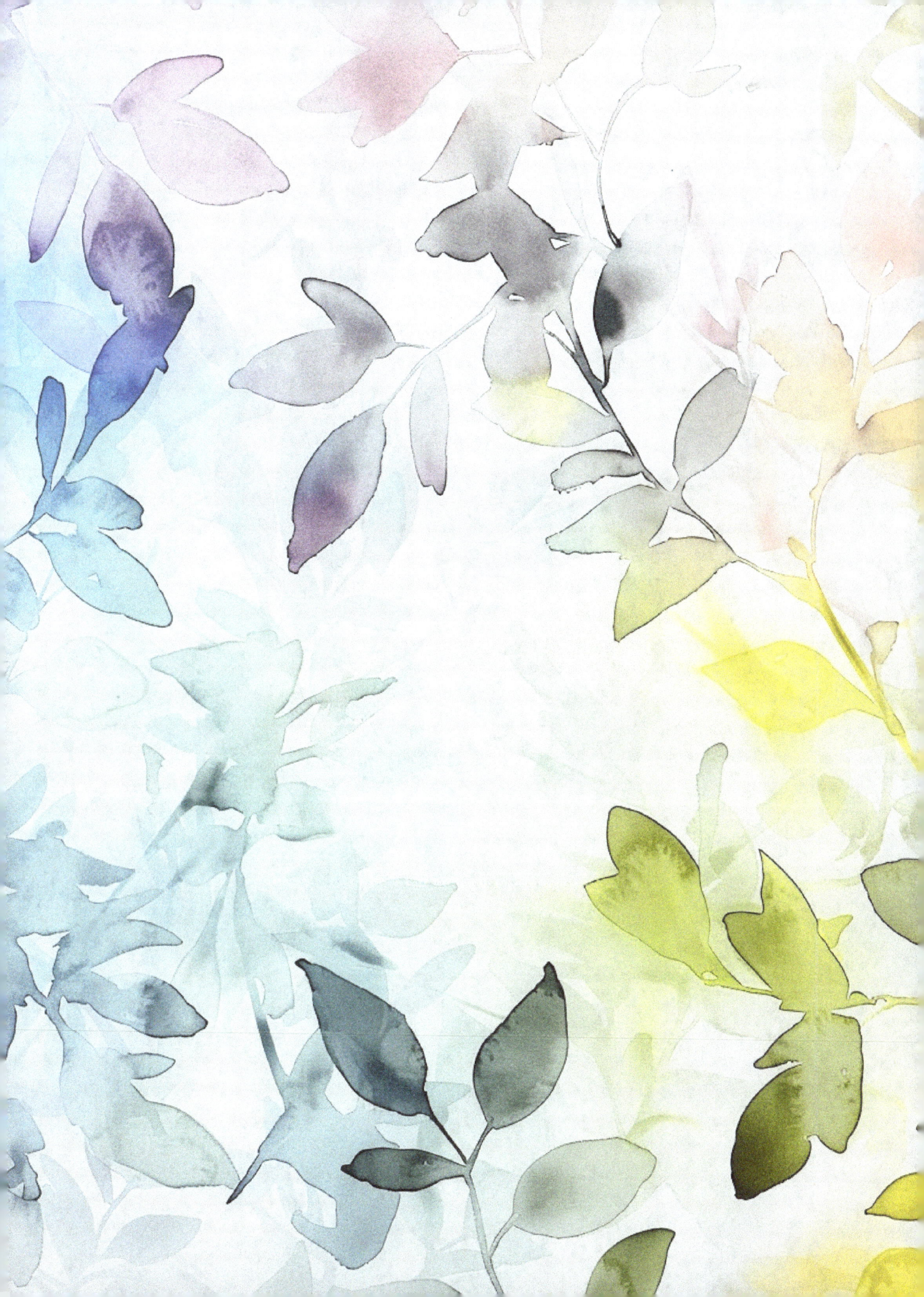

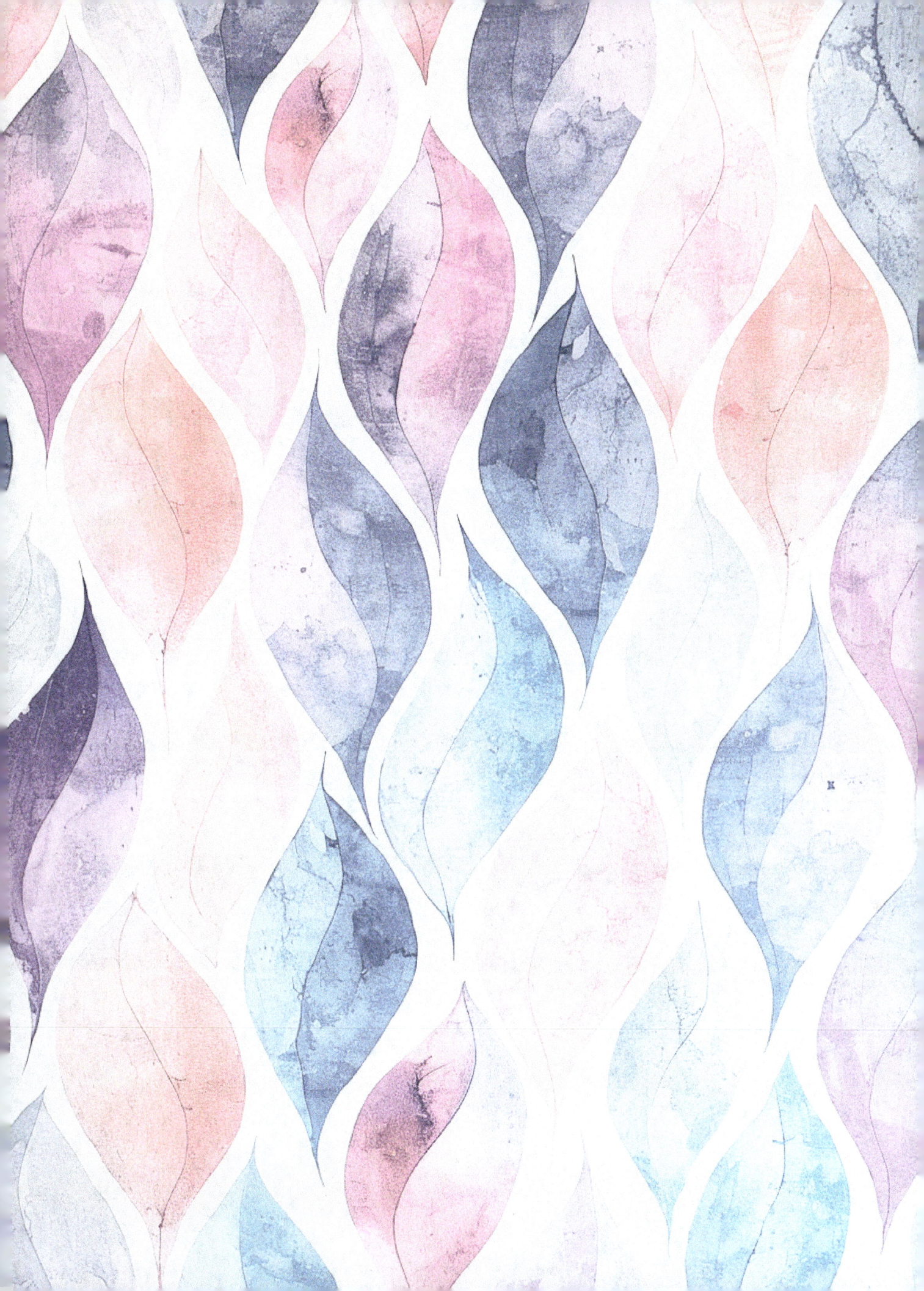

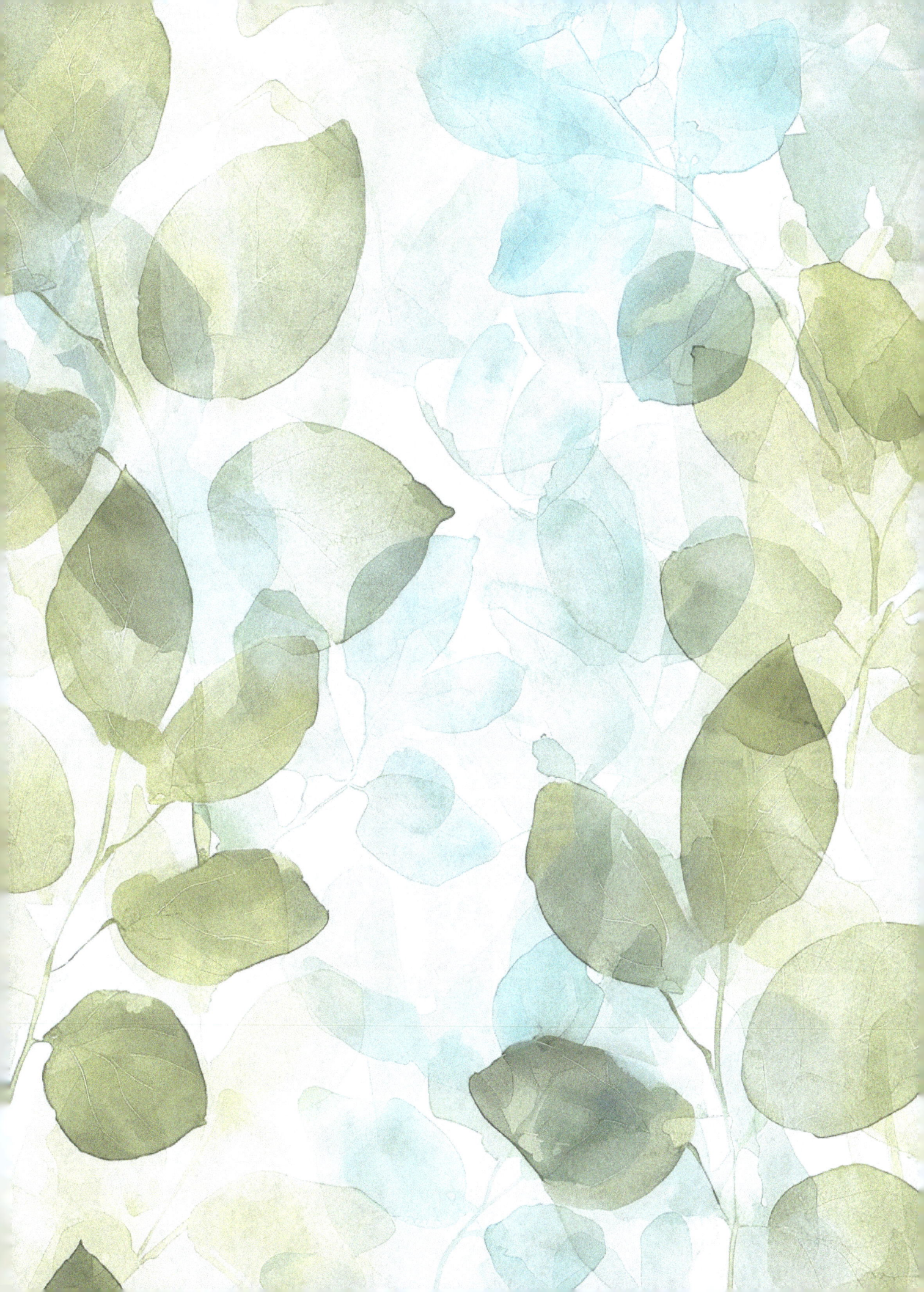

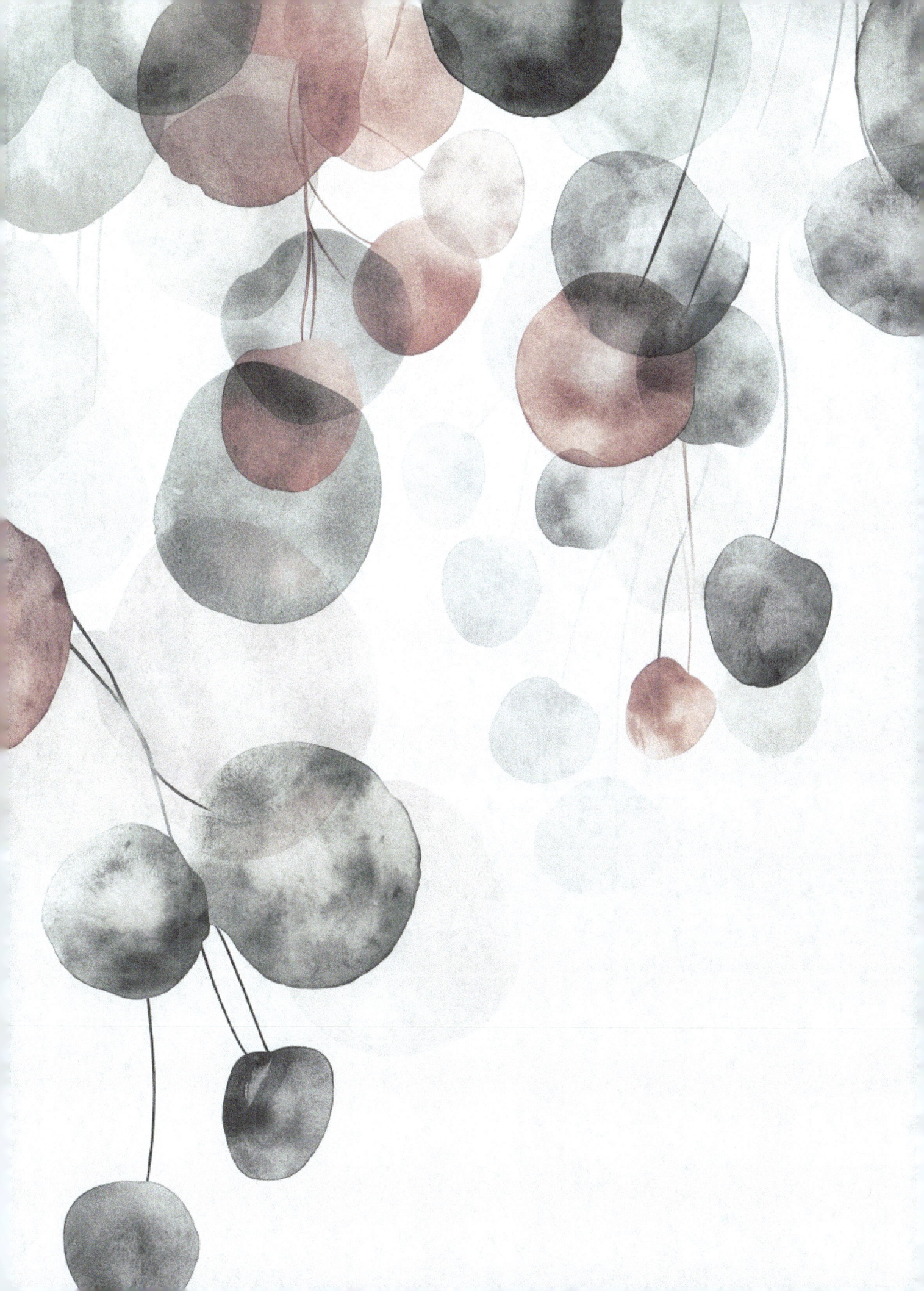

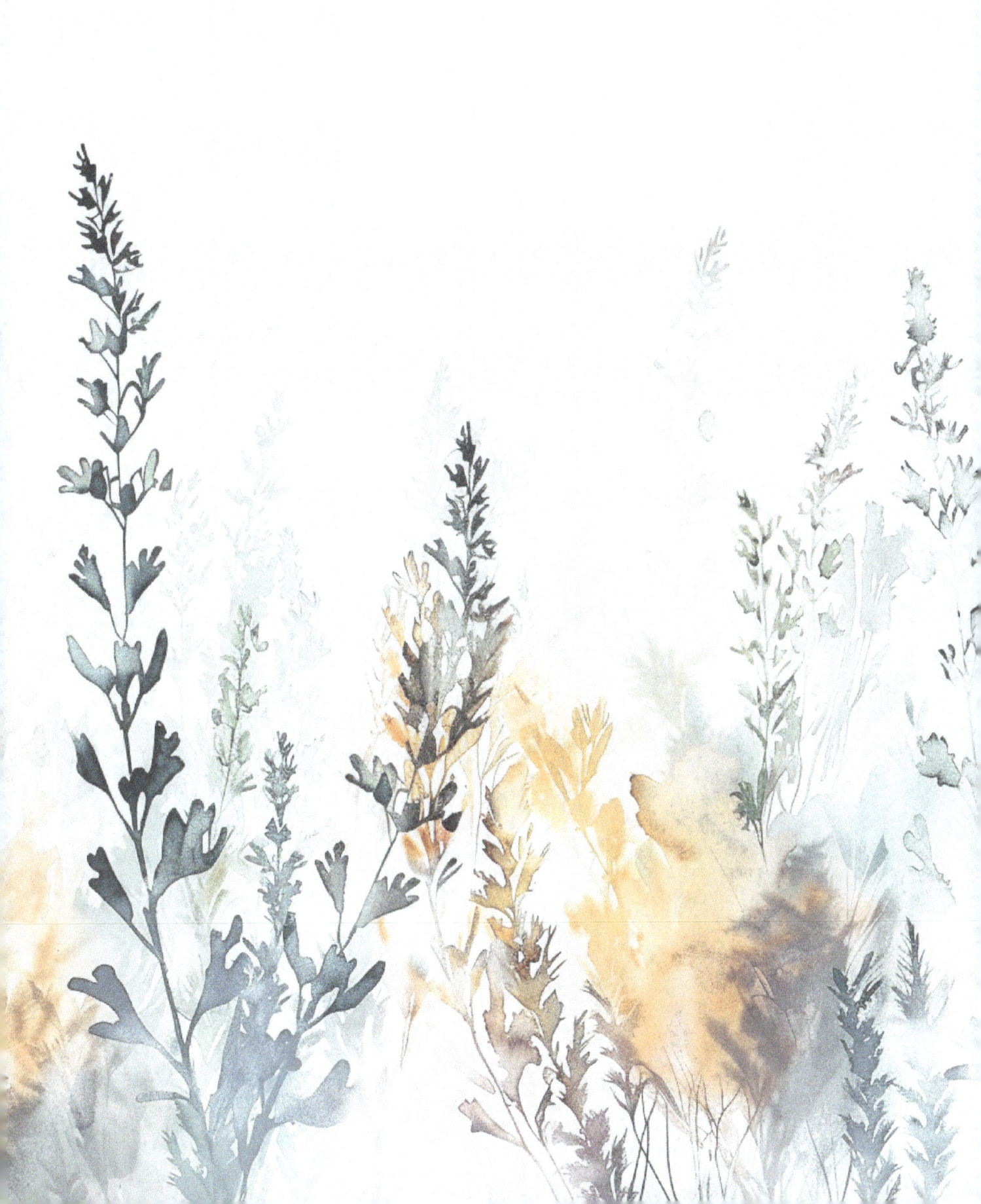

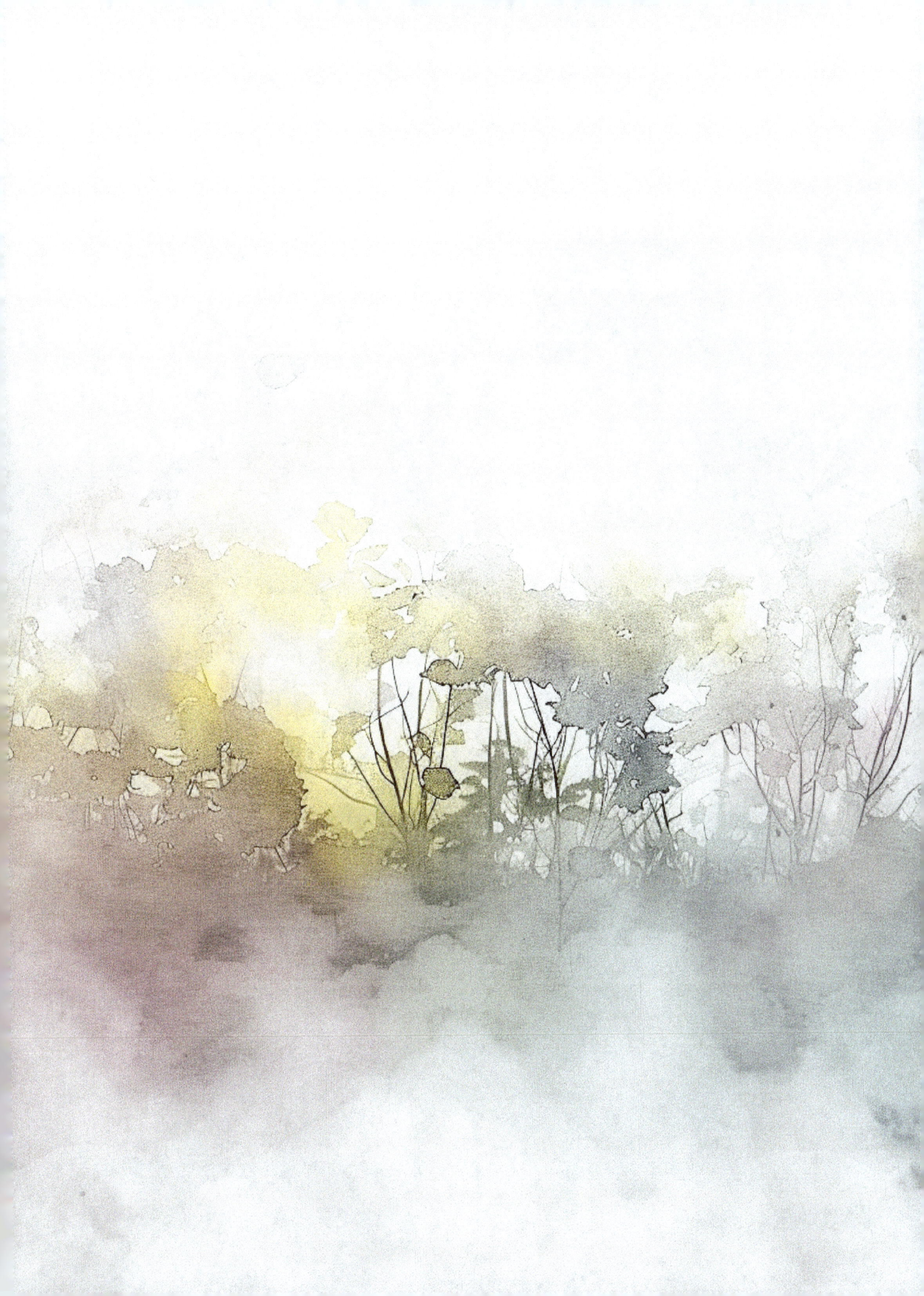

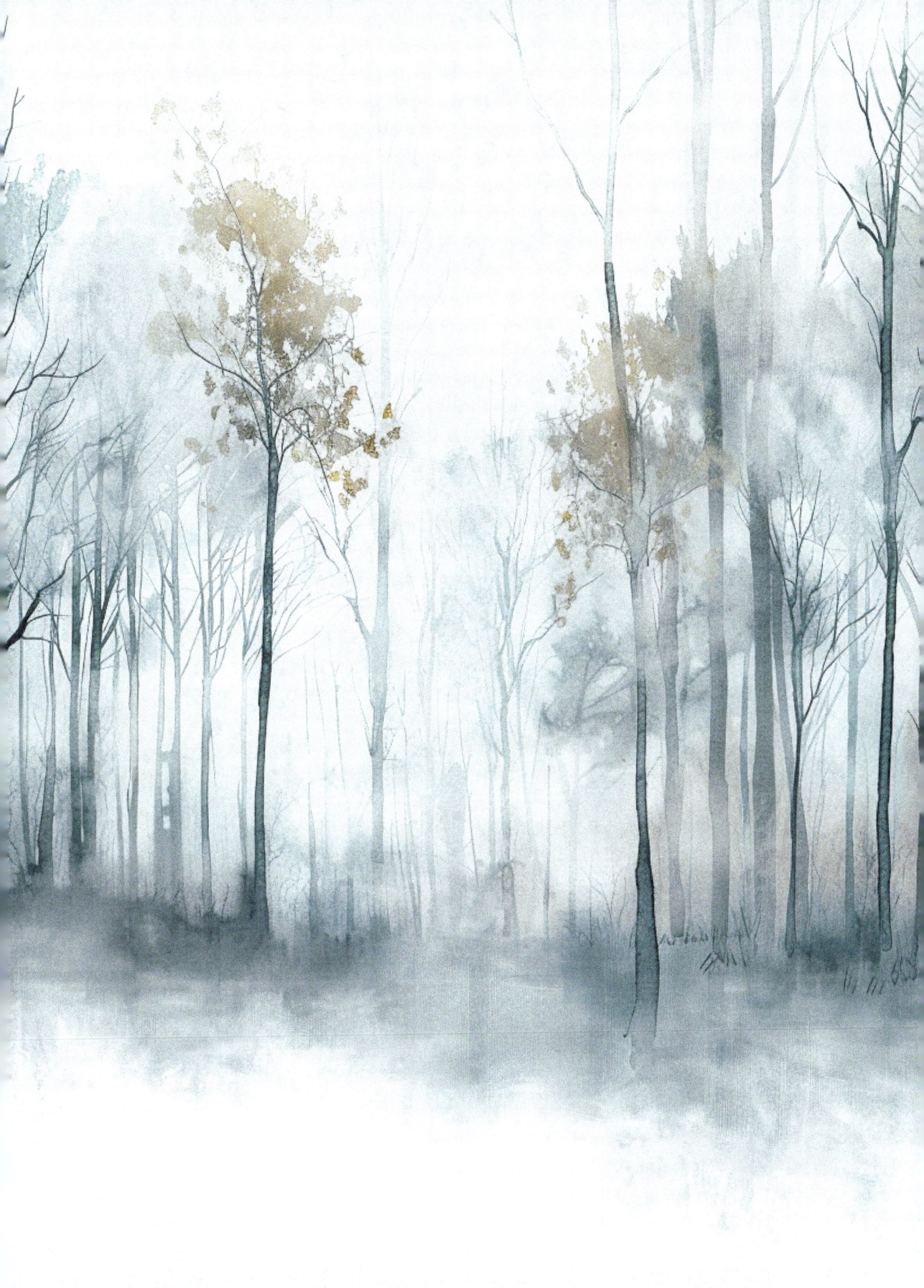

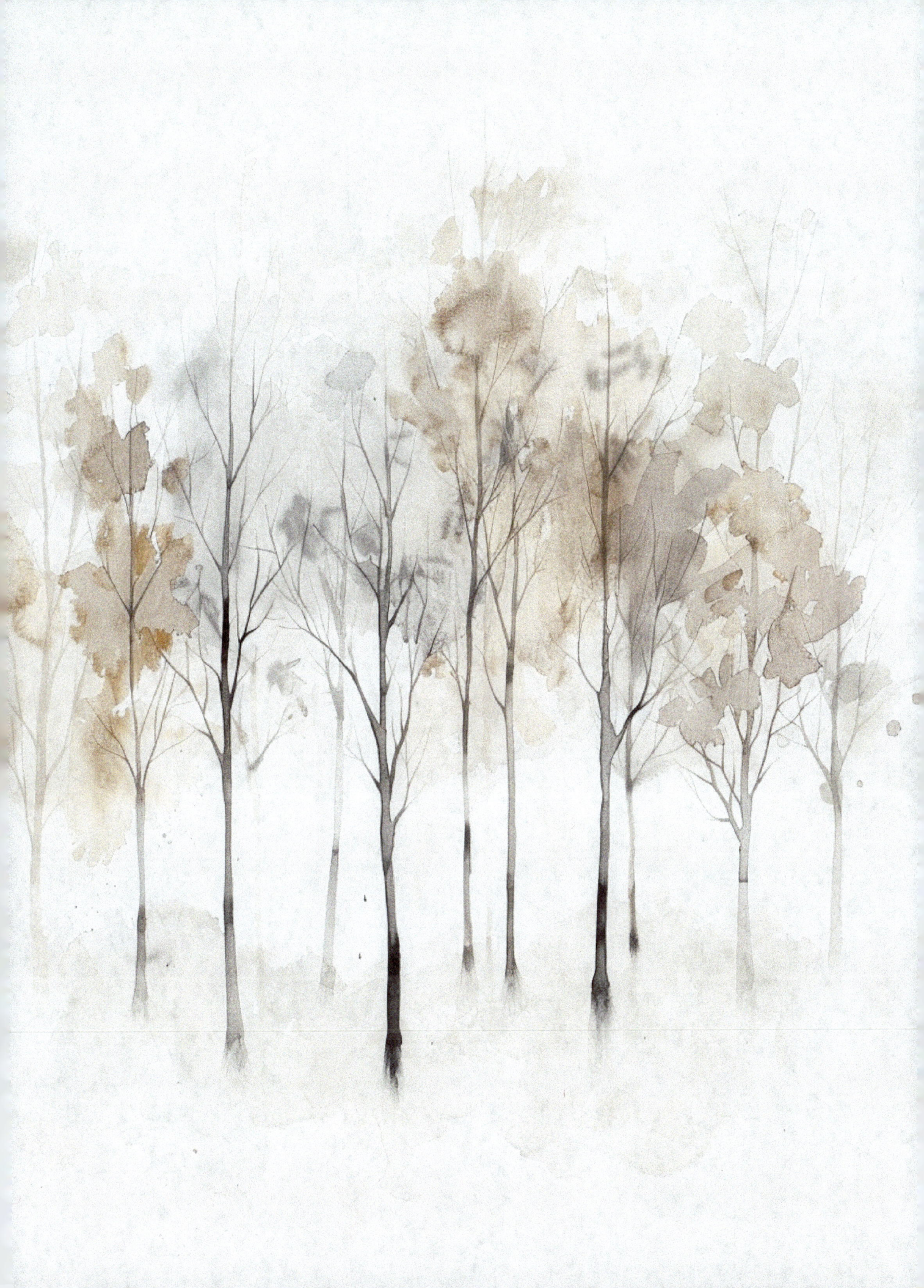

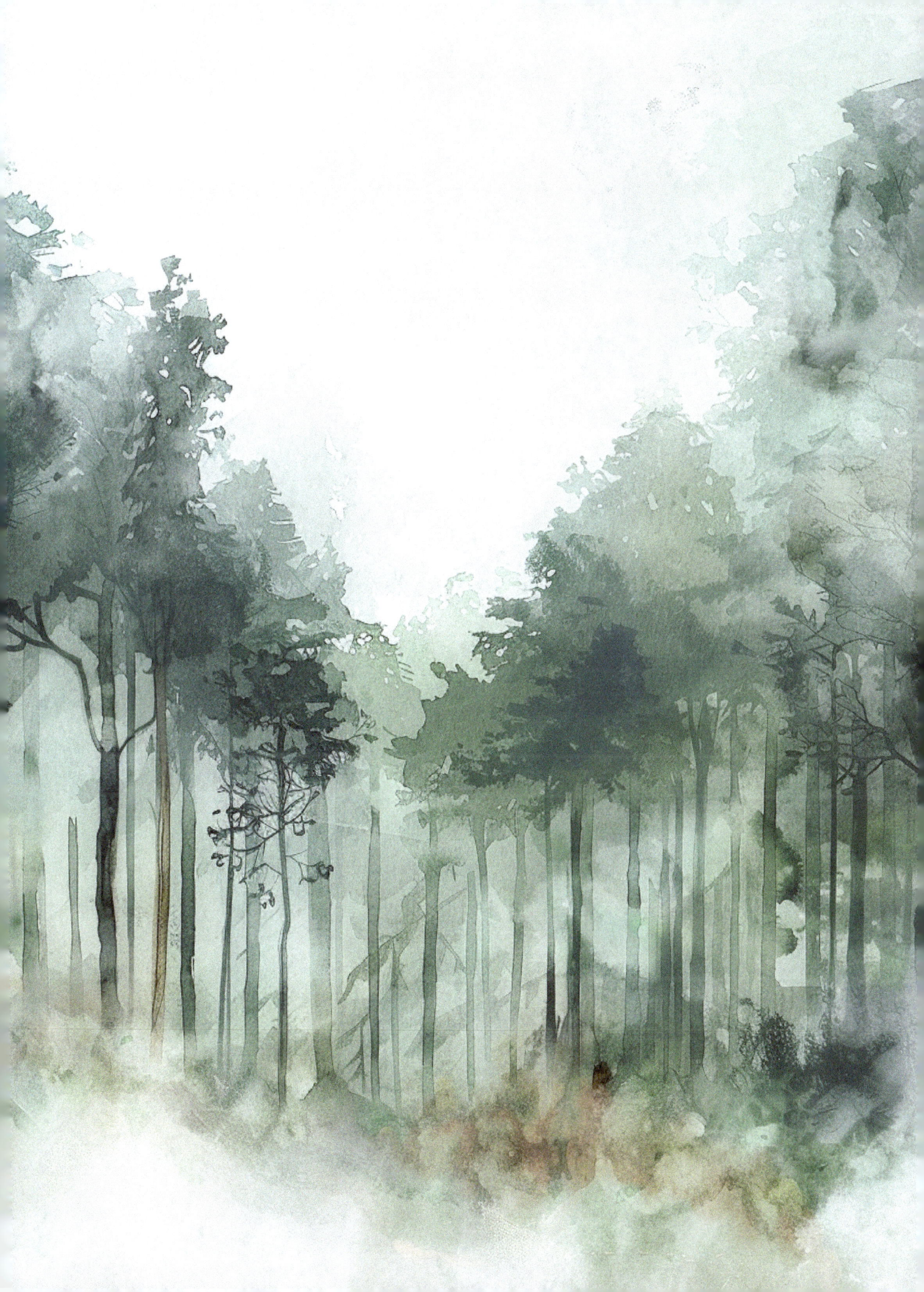

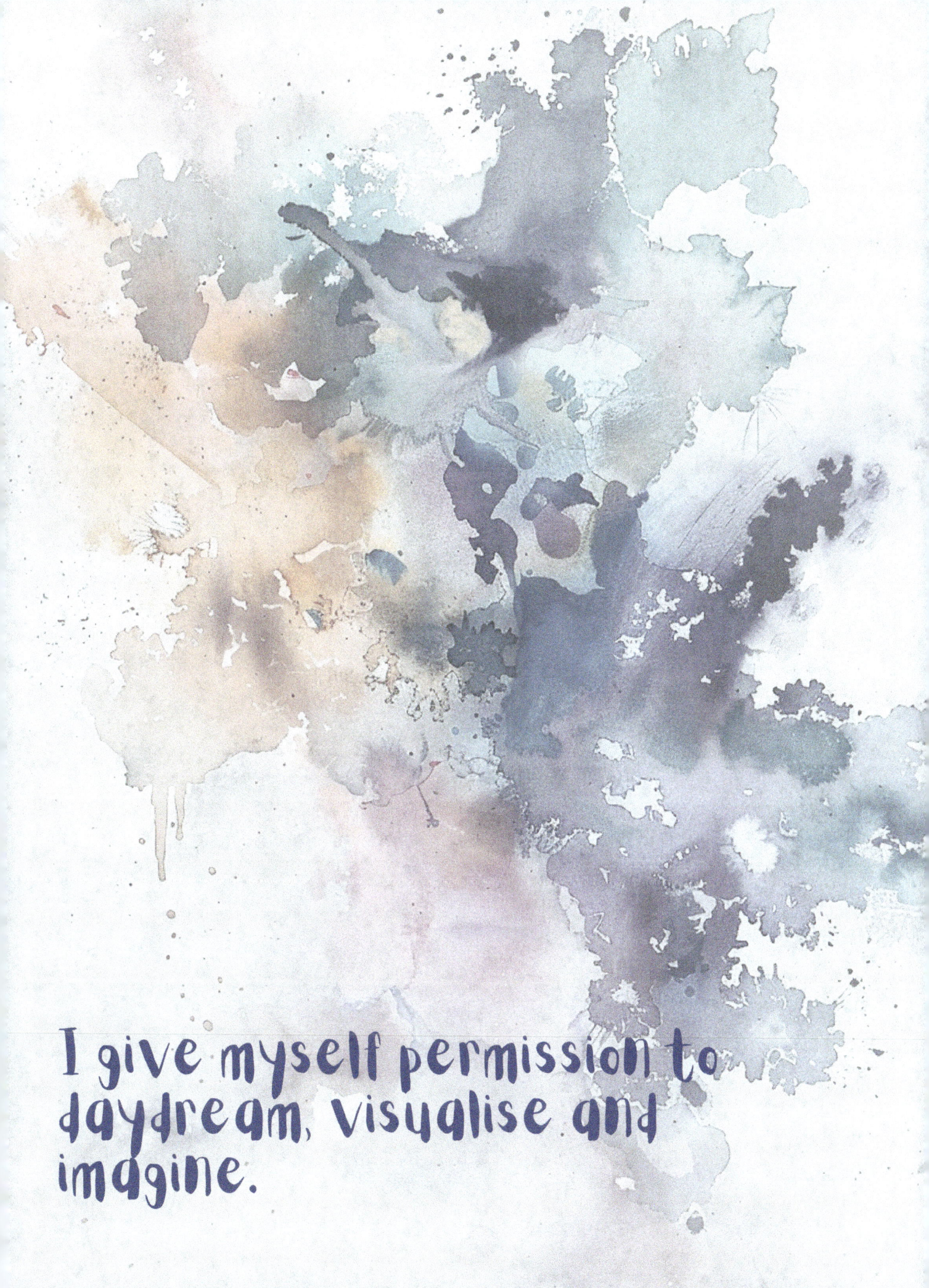

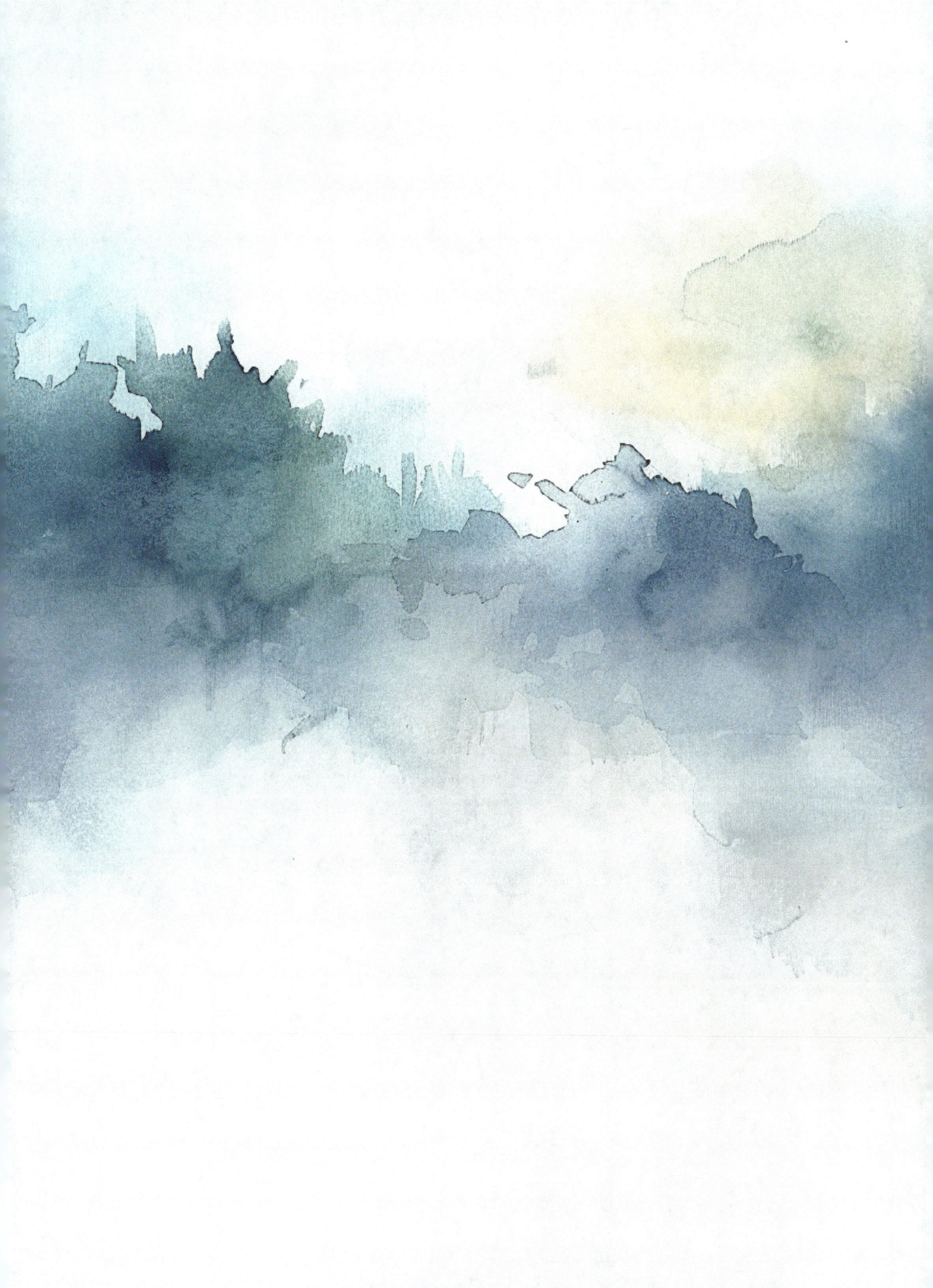

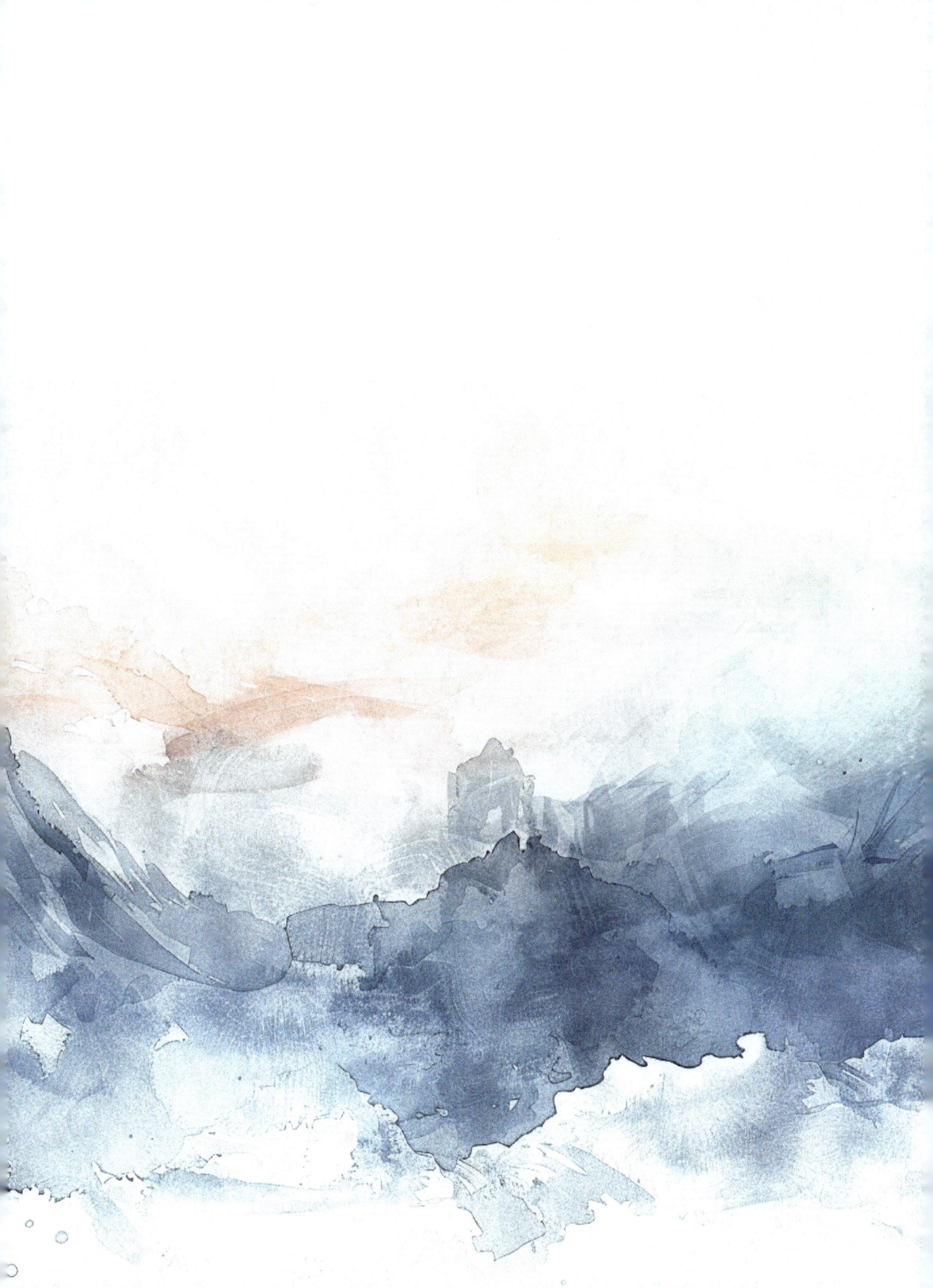

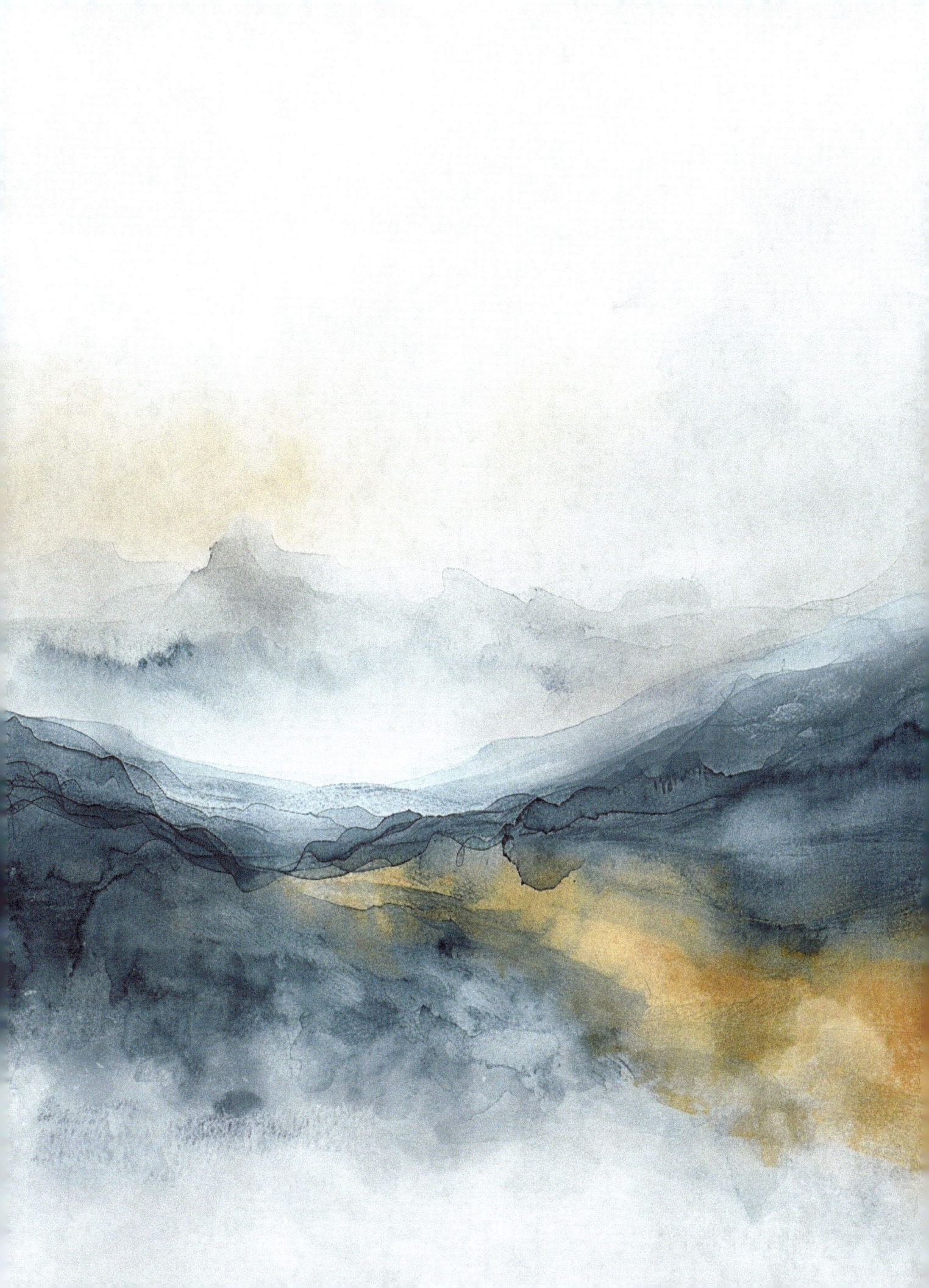

www.ingramcontent.com/pod-product-compliance
Lightning Source LLC
Chambersburg PA
CBHW082217220526
45470CB00010B/3207